Psychological Concepts and Psychotherapy in *Yoga Darśana*

By

Dr. Surinder Kaur

Siddharth Arya, MD

Amazon Books, USA

in association with

Indian Foundation for Vedic Science

1051, Sector-1, Rohtak, Haryana, India Ph: 01262-292580
(Rohtak) Delhi Contact No. 09313033917; 09650183260
Email: vedicscience@gmail.com
Website : www.vedascience.com

Second Edition

Kali era: 5115 (c. 2014)

Kalpa era : 1,97,29,49,115

Brahma era: 15,55,21,97,29,49,115

ISBN 81-87710-667

Contents

Introduction

Six philosophical thoughts, most often called as *Ṣaḍ Darśanas* of ancient India are the help books to understand the different aspects of the comprehensive knowledge enshrined in the Vedas. These six *Darśanas* are not different from Vedas, but the part and parcel of the long Vedic tradition of India. That is why, these books are called as *Āstika* (theist) *Darśanas* as they are pro-Vedas or say follow the guidelines of the Vedas. The philosophical thoughts developed other than these were called as *Nāstika Darśanas* or the philosophical thoughts developed disregarding the guidelines of the Vedas. The terms *Āstika* and *Nāstika* denote respectively pro-vedas and anti-Vedas. *Yoga Darśana* deals with the spiritual/metaphysical aspect of creation. Its main objective is to help human beings to develop themselves to the extent as to realise the Supreme Power/God.

Yoga is the science of Psycho-engineering. Just as physical sciences and technologies involve kinetic and potential energies for their operation, similarly science of psycho-engineering and māntrika technology developed in ancient India was based on Bhāvanā Sanskāra or psychic energy. *Yogadarśana* teaches us as to how to pool the psychic energy and utilize it in achieving various siddhis or divine powers. Yoga enables one to command over one's mental functions or processes. It helps us to develop a particular type of feeling suited to one's life. For instance, to make the life pleasurable, calm smooth and tensionless, it helps to develop a niṣkāma karma feeling, a feeling which inspires an individual to do altruistic welfare activities which are targeted for larger interest of society and not for individual interests. Such tendency if developed leads one towards the spirituality rather than materialism. The present book is a humble attempt to delve deep into the various psychological concepts dealt with in

Yogadarśana and to find out the relevance of psychotherapy available in *Yogadarśana* in the treatment of present day psychological disorders distressing the humanity at large.

Dr. Surinder Kaur
Siddharth Arya, MD
3005 N Kolmar Ave # 2
Chicago IL-60641

1

Concept of Intelligence

Ancient Indian philosophers made in-depth studies regarding the intelligence and came to the conclusion that intelligence is to have a confirmed knowledge of the objects or stimulus.

adhyavasāyātmikā buddhi

Where there is no confirmation, there can be no intelligence. In other words, unconfirming, perplexing, wavering (i.e. what to do or what not) situations or lack of decision making is not an intelligence. Modern psychologists have not considered intelligence in above respect. Rather they emphasized more on the factors of intelligence. Spearman, postulates a two factor theory. According to him, there are two types of intelligence, viz. general and specific. General intelligence deals with general ability, specific with specific ability. Wechsler finds intelligence as an ability to think rationally, to deal effectively and to act purposefully.

Spearman, has emphasized on the types of Intelligence and Wechsler on the outcome of intelligence, since if you have the power of decision making you will think rationally and deal effectively. Intelligence as having multi-factors has been specified by L.L. Thrustone and J.P. Guilford. Vermon in his hierarchical theory specifies that intelligence is like a pyramid. At the top of pyramid is Spearman's general intelligence underneath it are specific ability factors like Thurstone's primary mental abilities. Bottom of that lies Spearman's highly specific abilities. Recently psychologists have started describing intelligence as the power of quick decision making which was already defined by *Yoga Darśana* (*YD*) in the remotest past. As per *Yoga Darśana*, *adhyavasāyātmikā buddhi* can endow one with the capacity of quick decision making.

The Vedic scholiasts not only defined the intelligence, but descried *Yoga* as a pragmatic method to brighten the intelligence further and further till purity is attained in the form of *ṛtambharā prajñā.*

Modern psychologists earlier thought intelligence to be a time bound process. According to some, intelligence increases till the age of 16 only. According to others, it keeps on growing till the end of life and deteriorates only just before the death.

Yoga psychology doesn't end here. It emphasizes upon sharpening of intelligence. According to *Yoga*, the perfection of *nirvitarka samādhi,* helps sharpening or refinement of the intelligence. The intelligence thus sharpened/refined is called as *ṛtambharā prajñā.*

ṛtambharā tatra prajñā (*YD.* 1.48)

As a result of *ṛtambharā prajñā,* an individual is able to know the truth directly without help of language or thought. He obtains the knowledge of things or objects in his surrounding directly without an education, learning or experience whatsoever. The direct attainment of knowledge is known as realization or revelation. In Sanskrit-terms, it is called *Sākṣātkaraṇa.* In the beginning of creation, there were Ṛṣis who attained perfection of *Nirvitarka Samādhi* and so they were able to reveal or realize knowledge directly. The Vedas are said to be the results of efforts of such Ṛṣis.

Patañjali himself speaks of the peculiar characteristics of *ṛtambharā prajñā.* According to him :

śrutānumāna prajñābhyāmanyaviṣayā viśeṣārthatvāt

(*YD.* 1.49)

"The knowledge obtained due to *ṛtambharā prajñā* is different from the one received through words (heard or seen) or inference because it relates to a specific object or absolute reality or consciousness or God."

Through words or inference one can have knowledge of material things, but the knowledge of absolute reality or God can not be attained through words or inference. It can only be realized and the realization is possible only after attainment of the state or *ṛtambharā prajñā.*

Upaniṣads have also detailed this fact as under :

nahi tarkyeṇa eṣa labhya tamaiveṣa labhya yamaiveṣa vṛṇute.

As it has already been stated all sort of knowledge when received through words or inference or otherwise leaves its imprints on minds. These imprints are coded in the mind after knowledge is obtained through perception, inference etc. But once the *ṛtambharā prajñā* is developed and knowledge obtained due to *ṛtambharā prajñā* is impressed upon mind, imprints of other sets of knowledge are effaced or erased.

tajjaḥsaṁskāro'nyasaṁskāraprātibandhī (*YD.* 1.50)

The impressions gained through *ṛtambharā prajñā* are considered to be the strongest ones. They are able to counteract all other impressions.

In fact, these psychological impressions are material behind the creation of organism. It is explicitly explained in the Vedānta psychology that the impressions are the seeds of creation.

Saṁskāra bijāt sṛṣṭi

Various types of impressions leads to various types of creations. For example, *Saṁskāra,* the impressions of birds will lead one to the life of birds, of animals to animals, of insects to insects, of trees to trees.

It, however may be pointed out here that absence of impressions will lead to the absence of life, since there can be no plant without seeds.

So development of *ṛtambharā prajñā* is not the end of life, since *ṛtambharā prajñā* also leaves its impressions on the mind. The stage of *ṛtambharā prajñā* is the stage of *Saṁprajñāta Samādhī.* This *Saṁprajñāta Samādhī* does not leave an individual seedless or impressionless. Hence attainment of *Mokṣa* is not possible at this level. For attainment of *Mokṣa*, the stage of seedlessness or impressionlessness is must. Such a stage also occurs after some time the *ṛtambharā prajñā* is developed. And this stage of impressionlessness leads an individual toward

Nirbīja Samādhi or *Asaṁprajñāta Samādhī.*

tasyāpi nirodhe sarvanirodhānnīrbijaḥ samādhī (*YD.* 1.51)

At this stage the individuated consciousness is merged into universal consciousness. This may be called in psychological terms, as universalization of an individuated consciousness. This is more often than not is called as Mokṣa or Kaivalya.

2

Concept of Memory

Memory has been described in *Yoga Darśana* as one among the five primary mental functions.

According to Patañjali, memory is non-forgetting the perceived/experienced/or realized facts.

anubhūta viṣayāsampramaṣaḥ smṛtiḥ (*YD.* 1.11)

Here the word non-forgetting is important. It points to the desirability of a selective memory.

Yoga philosopher Patañjali's definition of memory, i.e. non-forgetting an experienced knowledge or fact clearly shows that memory consists of recalling a past experience which has been retained in mind. It involves retention and recall.

Process of Memory: Memory according to Patañjali may be divided into following parts :

1. *Anubhava*: First part of the process of memory is *Anubhava. Anubhava* is gained through perceiving a fact. In fact *abubhava* is a sort of learning consisted in perceiving facts.

2. *Saṁskāra: Saṁskāra* is the second part of memory. Perceived or experienced knowledge or facts are impressed upon mind in the form of *saṁskāras* or *karmas* and retained there with forever.

3. Recall or unforgetting is the third part. It is reproduction. It consists in the revival of past experience.

Here regarding the second part of memory one can raise a question as to *saṁkāras* impressed upon mind are retained temporarily for a short period or forever. Answer of Patañjali in this regard is very simple. According to him *saṁskāras* are inseparable part of memory. In fact, memory is formed of *saṁskāras.* So *saṁskāras* are factors in memory. Once they are impressed upon mind, they are never written off. Mind is the part of eternal consciousness. It is continuous and carries the record of its memory and *saṁskāras* through successive births.

jātideśakālavyavahitānāmapyānantaryaṁsmṛtisaṁskārayorekrūpat vāt

(*YD.* 4.9)

So memory is an eternal process of mind. It can be recalled regardless of interruption of place, time or birth. This is why, we meet with people who are able to recall the memories of their past lives.

Contents of Memory

Sabda (word) *artha* (object or reality) and knowledge (*jñāna*, i.e. mental awareness of things and words) are the contents of memory. It may exist either in terms of words, or objects (meaning) or in terms of knowledge of the existence of words or objects.

So long as memory has all the three contents, *Yoga* practitioner is able to meditate on these three taken together, i.e. an object, the word and the knowledge of that object or word.

So his meditation is related to or conditioned by and directed to an integration of these three. Suppose he concentrates on *Iśvara.* There is a name *Auma* or some other word for him. There is the reality called *Iśvara*, the presence, with his attributes or non-attributes and there is knowledge that he is there. Thus his concentration is on three-in-one and the attainment of this one is the direction in which he moves through *savitark samādhi.*

tatra śabdārthavikalpaiḥsaṁkīrṇā savitrkā samāpatti (*YD.* 1.42)

'*Samādhi* practised with words, meaning (object), and knowledge is known as *savitrkā samāpatti.*'

Clearance of Memory

The actual aim of Patañjali is to engineer one's mind for self realization, and the aim of self realization cannot be attained through *savitarkā smāpatti.* A practitioner has to move from *savitrkā samāpatti* to *nirvitarkā samāpatti.* Movement from *savitrkā samāpatti* to *nirvitarkā samāpatti* is not possible until and unless the memory is cleared of the above discussed contents. This process is known as clearance of memory or purification of memory. Memory can thus be cleared or purified with the help of mind meditating upon the object only i.e. *Iśvara,* leaving its word and knowledge out. After perfection in *savitarkā samādhi,* this type of practice for *nīrvītārkā samādhi* slowly purifies or clears mind of all contents.

According to Patañjali, on clearance of memory, in a state of mind as if void of itself, the light of the object alone shining, the state of meditation is called *nivitarkā samādhi.*

smṛtipariśuddhau svarūpaśunyevārtha mātra nirbhāsā nirvitarkā

(*YD.* 1.43)

The perfection of this *nirvitarkā samādhi* is said to be material in the achievement of spiritual light and bliss.

nirvicāravaiśāradye' dhyātma prāsādaḥ (*YD.* 1.47)

3

Cognition in *Yoga Darśana*

Just as the *Yāntrika* technology involves of kinetic and potential energies. Similarly *Māntrika* technology or mental technology developed in ancient India involved *Bhāvanā saṁskāra* or psychic-energy. *Yoga Darśana* tells about as to how to pool the psychic energy and utilize it in achieving various goals. *Yoga* enables one to command over one's mental functions or processes. It may help to develop a particular type of feeling suited to life so as to develop a *niṣkāma karma* feeling or a feeling where a particular action is done only for the sake of doing that action and not for the sake of material gains; a feeling where one is not much worried about material gains, but is satisfied with the efficient performance of his act.

Primary mental functions have been studied in the *Yoga Darśana* in the name of *Citta Vṛttis.* According to the Patañjali, there are five types of primary mental functions.

vṛttatyaḥ pañcatayaḥ kliṣṭā'kliṣṭāḥ (*YD.* 1.5)

They are us under

pramāṇa viparyaya vikalpa nidrāsmṛtayaḥ.

1. Cognition
2. False Cognition
3. Fiction
4. Sleep
5. Memory

1. Cognition: Cognition consists in knowing or knowledge of something. *Yoga* psychology calls it *pramāṇa.* Though *Nyāya Darśana* simply calls it *pramā* and the means through which the process of *pramā* (cognition) is accomplished is known in *Nyāya* as *prāmaṇa. Prāmakaraṇam pramāṇam.* 'Means of *pramā* is known as *pramāṇa.'*

So, there is a difference of opinion between the two philosophers on the issue of cognition. According to the Former, cognition is *pramāṇa* itself, but according to the latter cognition is *pramā* and *pramāṇas* are the means that lead to cognition. According to the *Patañjali,* there are three types of *pramāṇas* (cognition)

pratyakṣānumanāgamāḥ pramāṇāni. (*YD.* 1.7)

'Perception, inference and authority of senior in knowledge are cognition.'

1. Perception

2. Inference

3. Authority of senior in knowledge.

Before giving a detailed break up of the nature and definition of all the three types of cognition, it is necessary to point out here that the *Nyāya*-philosopher also enumerates among others as mentioned by Patañjali, *upamāna* (comparison) as the fourth means of cognition.

pratyakṣā numāno pamānāpto padeśāḥ pramāṇāni.

1. Perception: Consists in the presence of sense organs and a stimulus outside (*Indriyārtha sannikarṣa*). Other way round, it can be said that perception presupposes a sensation. *Nyāya* philosopher defines perception as

indriyārtha sanni karṣa janyaṁ jñānaṁ pratyakṣam

'The proximity of sensory organs with a stimulus leads to the process of perception.'

So perception is the first type of cognition based on sensation. Modern psychologists, however, consider sensation also as one kind of cognition. (Jadunath Sinhā 1948: 69, 100).

On the other hand ancient Indian scholars do not take sensation as a form of cognition. Rather they consider it as a basic factor or a priory to the perception or say element in perception.

2. Inference: Inference has been considered as the one type of cognition or means of cognition. For instance, if one see smoke, one can infer the presence of fire also.

yatra yatra dhūmaḥ tatra tatra vahniḥ.

'Where there is smoke there is fire.'

This type of reasoning also leads to the cognition. Hence inference can also be taken as a type of cognition or a means of cognition. In cognition by inference, the mental function of imagination is also involved.

3. Authority: Another type of method of cognition is authority or testimony of a person who is senior in knowledge. Cognition of everything can never take place directly or by direct experience. For the cognition of most of the things, one has to depend upon one's seniors who have already gained it from their seniors in tradition. So, cognition is also mostly gained in tradition from seniors by juniors. That is why, we are able to make advancement in our knowledge. Had we not gained it from the authority or testimony of seniors, there would have been no advancement as everyone would have to begin with the same beginning. Thus the knowledge would be repeated and duplicated, but it would not have advanced. It would rather have stagnated. Thus it is crystal clear from the foregoing discussion that the authority (*āgama*) is also one of the vital factors leading to cognition. In fact, testimony is the cognition of historical facts.

Earlier psychologists had no idea of this factor, but now the Indian philosophy is widely and extensively studied abroad, modern psychologists are hard pressed to talk about inference and testimony while dealing with the concepts of cognition.

4. Comparison (*Upamāna*) : Fourth factor helpful in cognition is comparison. Cognition is sometimes gained through comparison of one object with another. For instance, when one sees a *Nīla-gāya* in the jungle, he is able to recognize it on the comparison of experience of a cow already had by him in his vicinity.

In the cognition by comparison, the mental function of memory is also keenly involved, as for example, it is the reproduction of the past experience of cow that helps one in the cognition of *Nīla-gāya* in jungle.

Simply because of involvement of some mental function or another, the involved function cannot be termed as form of that function. This is what has been done by the modern psychologists in case of the mental functions of memory and imagination on account of their involvement in the mental function of cognition by way of inference and comparison. However ancient Indian psychologists did not include these into the forms of cognition.

The above said kinds of cognition are attained in normal course of life by individuals. Cognition of large number of objects or things is not possible. For instance, we can have the sensation of only those objects or things which are within the sensory range of our sense- organs, so there perception is also possible. But sometimes, the objects or things due to their location or size do not come within the range of our sensation or sensory power of our sense-organs, e.g. our eye can see objects within a particular range, our ears can hear up to a particular range, our nose can smell up to a limited distance, our skin can have sensation only of the objects that are closeted with it; we can taste only the things that are inserted into our mouth.

In other words one can say, an individual has no power of extra-sensory perception. Here it is necessary to point out that scope of *Yoga* starts where the range of sensory perception ends. *Yoga* deals with the extra-sensory perception. It explains a technique as to how to develop the power of extra-sensory perception. It explains as how an individual can have an extra-sensory perception of the things located at far off places or intervened by some other object or objects having atomic size and ultimately the extra-sensory perception (or realization) of self or individuated consciousness in the from of universal consciousness.

Yoga endows the practitioner with the divine sight, divine audition, divine olfaction, divine skin-sensation and divine taste. It tells one as to how an individual endowed with divine sight sees the objects intervened by some bigger object and objects located far off places or the objects which are atomic in size. It tell one as to how an individual endowed with divine audition, hears the sound from far off places; endowed with divine olfaction, smells odours of objects located at far off places; endowed with divine skin-sensation, feels the objects located at far off places; endowed with divine taste, tastes the distant things.

Perception is the realization of the presence of stimulus, but it may also be remembered that as per Vedic scholiasts realization of the absence of a stimulus already perceived is also a perception. For example, glass is not on the table or glass is missing is also a perception arose on account of the realization of the absence of stimulus.

Sensation (*Indriyārtha sannikarṣa*): Ancient Indian psychologists have defined nothing as sensation. In fact, they talk about *Indriyārtha sannikarṣa* i.e. the proximity of sense-organs with the stimulus. When this proximity of stimuli with respective sense-organs is realized in mind, it becomes perception or say converted into perception. So long as it (the proximity) is not realized, *Indriyārtha sannikarṣa* remains only the vague concept. It has nothing to do with the perception. So *Indriyārtha sannikarṣ a* is the most elementary material for the perception. In fact, it is the element in perception

Sensation is nothing but only a hypothetical concept. It is indeed a psychological myth as is had by Dr. Ward. (Jadunath Sinha, 1948:101)

According to ancient Indian scholiasts sensation as such is nothing but the realization of the presence of a stimulus or proximity of a stimulus with the sense organs.

Sensation of hunger and thirst: Hunger and thirst are also perceived through skin-sensation on account of the absence of stimuli inside the body. So, as per Indian psychology, they can be perceived through skin-sensation. Keeping in view this fact, *Vaiśeṣikas* also enumerate *abhāva* or absence of a stimulus or object among the various types of object.

This way perception may also be classified as positive and negative perception.

1. Positive perception arising out of the realization of the presence of a stimuli,

2. Negative perception arising out of the realization of the absence of a stimulus.

Stimulus (*Artha or Dravya*): Stimulus is one of the essential factors for cognition. It may exist outside or inside the organism. So, it may be either external or internal to the organism. It acts upon the receptors or sense-organs. It is always in the form of an object or a thing. But the Indian scholiasts particularly later philosophers of *Vaiśeṣika* school have taken into account *abhāva* or 'absence of a stimulus' as the form of a stimulus.

Just as the presence of a stimulus act upon a receptor or sense organ, similarly absence of a stimulus already experienced by an individual also act upon our receptors or sense organs.

This is why, we often hear a negative response from the individuals. For instance, glass is missing. Today we did not hear the same old music. The smell of an inscence stick has stopped coming. I would like to eat mango, etc. These types of responses by individuals support the hypothesis of an *abhāva* or 'absence of an already experienced stimulus' as a stimulus.

Vaiśesikas have also enumerated several other *dravyas.* They may also be taken into account.

1. First, an object or a thing is called *artha.* So can we have any solid object or thing as a stimulus to act upon our receptors or sense-organs.

2. *Guṇas* or qualities have been enumerated as the second type of stimulus. All sorts of qualities (enumerated about 24 in numbers) e.g. colours, sounds, tastes, smells, pressures, heat, cold, etc. also act upon individual's sense-organs as stimulus. The modern psychologists classify the sensations of qualities as special sensations (Jadunath Sinha, 1948 : 110)

3. *Karma* or action has been classified as the third type of

stimulus. Five types of movements such as *utkṣepaṇa* 'to throw up', *avakuñcana* 'to contract' etc. have been enumerated as five actions.

Sensations produced by various kinds of movements are called motor or kinesthetic sensations by the modern psychologists.

4. The fourth type of stimulus visualized by the Indian scholiasts is the universalization or generalization of an individuated object. They call it *sāmānya* i.e. the universal or general object. We may have the realization of universal objects also such as consciousness. This is the main goal of the *Yoga. Yoga* philosophy doesn't deal with any sensation counted so far by modern psychologists special or kinesthetic, but it deals only with the universal sensation. Thus *Yoga* is not a study of sensory process or else, but it is a method or technique that may activate the sensory process to lead an individual towards universal sensation.

5. Fifth object is *Viśeṣa* or individuated one. Any object is called individuated which has some distinct character as compared to the others of the same class. We may have the sensation of objects in general as well as in particular.

The object of *Yoga* is individuated-self. It starts from the sensation of individuated self (consciousness) ultimately reaching the sensation of universal-self or universal consciousness through various phases of concentration and contemplation.

6. Sixth object is *abhāva*, as already, discussed above, *abhāva* or absence of an experienced object also acts as a stimulus. The organic sensation of hunger and thirst are caused by the *abhāva dravya* through skin-sensation, though modern psychologists have named them as organic sensations caused by physiological changes originating in the organism itself. (Jadunath 1948 : 103). They call the physiological changes as intra-organic stimuli. For instance, according to them, muscular contractions in the walls of stomach produce sensation of hunger. Dryness of the palate produces sensation of thirst.

In fact, as stated in the light of Indian point of view, these are nothing else, but the sensation of the absence of a stimuli located inside the body. For example the absence of water inside the body leads to the sensation of thirst. Similarly, absence of consumed meals leads to the sensation of hunger. Moreover, sensation of cuts, burns, sores, bruises, etc. are also a sort of skin-sensation caused by the presence or proximity of stimuli with the skin.

Stimulus and Response : According to Patañjali, the *Yoga* philosopher, the mental process of cognition as well as other such as false-cognition, imagination, sleep and memory leads to vital feelings, e.g. comfort or discomfort.

vṛttayaḥ pañcatayyaḥ kliṣṭā'kliṣṭāḥ.

'Mental processes are painless or comfortable as well as painful or uncomfortable.

In case of cognition, it depends upon the stimulus which is responded to by the organism or individual.

In fact, comfort and discomfort are not the organic sensations, to be dealt with separately, as is done by modern psychologists (Jadunath 1948: 110). They are the sort of response of an organism/individual towards the stimuli acting upon his receptors or sense-organs.

The positive responses are taken as comfortable and negative responses as uncomfortable or painful. So comfort and discomfort are not sensations, but qualify the sensations. All the sensations can either be comfortable or uncomfortable depending upon their stimuli. Comfortable sensations are always welcomed on the other hand uncomfortable sensations are always avoided.

According to Patañjali sensation of Universal consciousness is quite blissful.

Here it may be pointed out that the consciousness is a stimulus of the very lowest degree of intensity. So, it cannot produce sensations in our mind. Not only this, we have many other stimuli of low degrees of intensity of which we have no sensation. For instance a very faint sound, a very faint light, a very faint odour fail altogether to produce a sensation, what to say of the consciousness. In fact, the sensory power of our sense-organs is limited. An individual has a particular range of sensibility. A stimulus of a particular intensity may produce sensation, neither a stimulus of higher intensity nor do the lower intensity produce sensation.

In view of the range of an individual sensibility being very particular, the modern psychologists often talks about increasing the stimulus up to the level of its being able to produce an appreciable sensation. The Weber Fechner law is the result of the hypothesis that the range of sensibility of an organism being particular or not the subject of change, the only way out is to increase the stimulus up to the level of appreciable sensation. If the Ameba is too small to produce vital sensation, its size may be increased with the help of binocular up to the level it may produce sensation in the mind.

On the other hand so far as the sensation of universal consciousness is concerned, the situation is quite odd and reverse. We have no instrument which can increase 'This stimulus' in terms of size or volume. Hence under the circumstances when the stimulus remains unchanged and of the same lowest intensity, Patañjali comes forward with the technique of *Yoga*. According to him, our range of sensitivity is not static, it can also be increased if the need be. So, he unravels the secrets of *Yoga*. Through *Yoga* one can increase the range of one's sensibility and attain the power what we more often than not call extra-sensory perception. Thus having acquired the extra-sensory power through the regular practice of *Yoga,* one is able to respond even to the stimulus of lowest degree of intensity and his response is often described as blissful.

Eventually on the basis of foregoing discussion, it can be summed up that *Yoga* is a technique. It doesn't study the mental process like that of Psychology. Rather it deals with as to how to engineer the mental process towards the desired end. Thus *Yoga* may be described as a subject of Psycho-engineering or a technical aspect of the science of Psychology.

4

Psychological Disorders And Their Cure

From the beginning of human society, people have suffered from sadness, mysterious symptoms, and bizarre behaviour. The physicians and healers on various parts of the Globe tried to classify these disorders, explain them, and cure them. Here it would be interesting to know as to how Patañjali, one of the dominating figure in the Indian wisdom, viewed these disorders. He associated them with the mental process of an Individual, which, according to him could be described as either comfortable / painless or uncomfortable / painful.

Vṛttayaḥ pañcatayyaḥ kliṣṭā'kliṭāḥ [*Yogadarśana* (YD) 1.5]

In fact, comfortable processes were described by him as the normal mental functions and uncomfortable processes as the malfunctions.

Uncomfortable or painful processes or malfunctions are further divided into five types, viz. *avidyā.* being first one followed by *asmitā, rāga, dveṣa* and *abhiniveśa.*

Avidyā is said to be the root cause of all others that follow it e.g. *asmitā, rāga, daveṣa and abhiniveśa.*

avidyā kṣetraṁuttreṣāṁ prasuptatanu vicchannodārāṇām

(*YD.* 2.4)

Avidyā, according to Patañjli is the sense of permanence in transient, of purity in the impure, of pleasure in displeasure of consciousness in unconscious.

anityā śuciduḥkhānātmasu nityaśuci sukhātmakhyātiravidyā

(*YD.* 2.5)

Thus the malfunctioning of mental process is identified by

Patañjali in utter confusion of opposites, of good and bad, truth and falsehood, pure and impure, permanent and temporary, conscious and unconscious, the essential and existential, etc. It is a confusion as much as a positive and negative, light and dark.

Avidyā causes possessiveness (vfLerk) to follow. *Asmitā* is thoroughly possessive state of mind. An individual becomes highly possessive. Patañjali describes this malfunction as follows :

dṛgdarśanaśaktyorekātmatevāsmitā (*YD.* 2.6)

Asmitā is the blending of an individual together with the objects.

Asmitā (possessiveness) further gives rise to attachment. The individual of possessive nature becomes highly attached to the objects. This attachment is a pleasurable experience. According to *Yoga* philosopher :

sukhānuśayī rāgaḥ (*YD.* 2.7)

'Attachment is the cause of pleasure.'

However, more and more attachment or intense attachment is often said to be the cause of aversion. Aversion or hatred is again very painful.

duḥkhānuśayī dveṣaḥ (*YD.* 2.8)

Last but not the least malfunction of mind is the development of anxiety disorder form of death phobia or desire to live forever *(abhiniveśa).*

svarasvāhī viduṣo'pi tathārūḍho'bhiniveśaḥ (*YD.* 2.9)

According to Patañjali, malfunctioning of mental process can be minimized with the help of some orientation programme popularly known as *Kriyā Yoga.*

samādhi bhāvanārthaḥ kleśtanūkaraṇārthaśca (*YD.* 2.2)

'*Kriya-Yoga* is for bringing about *Samādhi* and minimizing mental malfunctions (*Kleśas*).'

The orientation program or *Kriyā Yoga* is of three-fold. It includes observance of physical discipline counselling and above all faith.

tapaḥsvādhyāyeśvarapraṇidhānāni kriyāYogaḥ (*YD*. 2.1)

Physical discipline is described in terms of *tapaḥ*. *Tapaḥ* is austerity, hard discipline of body and its habits in order to facilitate change in behavior. It is always observed at the physical level. Counselling is described in terms of *svādhyāyaya*. It is always observed at the mental level. *Svādhyāya* is the self-analysis. It is development of insight into one's own self. It is a short of humanistic approach to therapy. It aims at sharpening the individual's self awareness. *Svādhyāya* is also pointer to the study of good works of literature on life and living, philosophy and ethics. It also includes counselling or *upadeśa* by the person who is well-read and quite senior in experience and khowledge.

Last factor of *Kriyā Yoga* is the faith. Faith is must for any short of treatment you receive for the remedy of your illness. In fact, faith means faith in God. Faith in God helps boost one's confidence and confidence is the key to success.

Thus the above given orientation programme is must for cessation of mental malfunctions (*Kleśa*).

If the mental malfunctions are not ceased, their further aggravation or development takes place into the form of various *cittavikṣepas*, what we call in modern psychological terms as Psychological disorders.

Pātañjali enumerates all these psychological disorders as:

vyādhistyānasaṁśayapramādālasyāviratibhrāntidarśanālabdhbhūmikatvānicittavikṣepāste'ntarāyāḥ (*YD*. 1.30)

First one is *vyādhi* or psychosomatic disorder. Suffering from this disorder an individual complaints sickness without any apparent organic cause.

Second disorder is *styāna* or *ālasya*. *Ālasya or styāna* denotes the disorder of affect like dullness, languor, sloth, drooping state, incompetence, spiritlessness, purposelessness and boredom indicating depression.

Third disorder is *Pramāda. Pramāda* denotes carelessness, casualness, drift, deliberate lack of commitment, and earnestness indicating a type of personality disorder.

Fourth one is enumerated as *anavasthitatva.* It may also be taken, in modern psychological terms, as another type of personality disorder. A person suffering from *anavasthitatva* will show his behaviour inconsistent with his words. He doesn't follow his own promises or obligations; he is perfectly willing to deceive and defraud other people; he is always an unstable person or unable to stay in a state.

Fifth one is enumerated as *avirati* which represents the obsessive-compulsive neurotic disorder. A person suffering from this disorder personally becomes indulged both at thought and action level.

Sixth disorder is *bhrāntidarśana* which may be taken for psychotic disorders having confusion, delusion, hallucination etc.

Seventh disorder is counted to be *alabdhabhūmikatva* i.e. inability to recognize objects and their meanings. Hysterical disorders may be represented by *alabdhabhūmikatva.*

Patañjali also reflects light on the psychophysiological symptoms of various types of psychological disorders. According to him, (*duḥkha*) i.e. sadness and *daurmanasya* (frustration), *aṅgameyajatva* (nervousness) and *śvāspraśvāsa* i.e. disturbed breathing are nothing but the psychological symptoms of various types of psychological disorders.

duḥkhadaurmanasyāṅgamejayatvaśvāsapraśvāsāvikṣ
epasahabhuvaḥ

(*YD.* 1.31)

For the information of our readers it may be mentioned that all types of psychological disorders have also been discussed in detail in the *Ayurveda.* The *Ayurveda* deals with all the psychological disorders in the name of *Manasrogas.*

Therapy for Various Psychological Disorders

Thousands of years back, when the rest of world was

grappling with these disorders in barbarous ways, Indian wisdom explored this field in depth and recognized the psychological disorders as mental illness, some curable and others hardly curable.

Ayurvedic seers suggested a herbal therapy for various psychological disorders. The present nature of the work does not allow the authors to go into the details thereof.

Here we shall present an account of therapeutic methods suggested by *Yogadarśana* for the treatment of Various psychological disorders.

Patañjali suggests the *Yoga* therapy as the single out treatment for the neurotic disorders discussed above.

Yoga Therapy

The *Yoga* therapy suggested by Pantañjali for the various types of psychological disorders consists of three parts :

1. Training of mind or meditation
2. Relaxation of mind
3. Third one is the training of breath or *prāṇāyām*, or relaxation of body.

Now we shall discuss all three parts of therapy suggested by Patañjali in detail :

1. Training of Mind or Meditation :

All the psychological disorders and physiological disorders affecting mind side by side can be counteracted or treated with the help of meditation.

tatpratiṣedhārtham ekatattvābhyāsaḥ *(YD 1.32)*

'To counteract these disorders, meditation should be practised.'

According to him, meditation is the best way to attain mental relaxation and thereby treating the disorders.

He himself explains the term meditation and the method of meditation. How can one practice meditation of the Principal reality / Supreme self or consciousness?

As to the question of what is meditation he explains meditation as to surrender oneself to almighty. How can one practice meditation of God or surrender to Him? He tells a very simple method. If you want to meditate upon Him or surrender yourself to Him, you should keep Him in your mind each and every second.

tajjapastadartha bhāvanam (*YD.* 1.28)

Now one may ask in what form or with what sign one can keep him in mind. Patañjali gives a very simple answer. According to him. *Aum* is the name. He may be referred to by His name *Aum.*

Tasya vācakaḥ praṇavaḥ (*YD.* 1.27)

2. Relaxation of mind

Relaxation of mind can be achieved through various

ways :

- First way is mental loosening up. One will feel relaxed if he gets out of mental roots. Patañjali in this regard states as under :

vītarāgaviṣayaṁ vā cittam

'If the mind becomes free from all passions and thoughts, the disorders may be counteracted.'

- Second way of mental relaxation is the undivided concentration or attention. The undivided attention can be generated in many ways. The mind may be directed to attend on one object or thought. According to Patañjali, a habit of mind to attend on one single point / object or thought brings about the relaxation of mind.

viṣayavatī vā pravṛttirutpannā manasaḥ

sthitir nibandhanī (*YD.* 1.35)

Mind may be directed, as per Patañjali, apart from attending on an external object to attend on one's own self. Directing concentration / attention on one's own self also leads to the relaxed state of mind.

viśokā vā jyotiṣmati

(*YD.* 1.36)

The attention may also be directed to some blissful knowledge revealed in the state of dream or sleep in order to attain relaxation of mind.

svapna nidrā jñānāvalam banaṁ vā. (*YD.* 1.38)

Or through concentration on choiced object, one may relax his mind.

yathābhimata dhyānādvā (*YD.* 1.39)

According to Patañjali mind may, for the purpose of concentration, be focused on any object ranging from smallest particle to the greatest and highest object.

paramāṇuparama mahttvānto'sya vaśikāra (*YD.* 1.40)

Thus all the three ways, mental loosening up or thoughtlessness of mind, undivided attention or concentration and meditation leads to mental relaxation which causes the end or smoothening of disorders.

3. Training of Breath or Prāṇāyāma

Third part of *Yoga* therapy is relaxation of body. Best way of relaxing the body is observance of prāṇāyāma or regulation and control of breath. There is a saying, sound body keeps a sound mind. If body is not relaxed, how can mind be without distractions and agitations. For relaxation of mind, relaxation of body is must. Disturbed breath is the symptom of mental agitation.

duḥkhadaurmansyāṅgamejayatvaśvāsapraśvāsāvikṣepa sahabhuvaḥ

(*YD.* 1.31)

Regulated and controlled breath will also lead to the peace of mind or mental relaxation.

pracchardana vighārṇābhyāṁ vā prāṇasya (*YD.* 1.34)

'By controlled and regulated inhalations and exhalations,

mind gets relaxed leading to the counteraction of disorders.'

Patañjali defines *prāṇāyāma* as :

tasminsati śvāsapraśvāsayorgativicchedaḥprāṇāyāmaḥ

'*Praṇāyāma* is the suspension of inhalation and exhalation by being in the state of some posture.'

According to Vyāsa, a commentator of *Yogadarśana*, when the *āsana* has been perfected, the suspension of inhaling external air, and that of exhaling the internal air i.e. suspension of either way, is *prāṇāyāma.*

Thus there are three types of *prāṇāyāma :* external, internal and stilled.

External *prāṇāyāma* is the suspension of exhalation. Internal *prāṇāyāma* is suspension of inhalation. Stilled *prāṇāyāma* is observed in absence of both the external and internal *prāṇāyāmas*, when breath is neither exhaled nor inhaled, but stilled as it is and where it is, it is called *stambavṛtti* or stilled *prāṇāyāma.*

bāhyābhyantara stambhavṛttirdeśakālasaṁkhyābhiḥ

pridṛṣṭo dīrgha sūkṣamāḥ (*YD.*1.50)

Prāṇāyāma is external, internal and stilled. It may be long or subtle when measured in space, time and numbers.

The above mentioned three types of *prāṇāyāma* were later referred to as *recaka,* the external, as *puraka,* the internal and the one as *kumbhaka.*

In fact *kumbhaka* or *stambhavṛtti* is suspension of breath in between inhalation and exhalation.

Patañjali also takes into account the fourth type of *prāṇāyāma.*

The three types of *prāṇāyāmas* discussed above requires inhalation and exhalation. But the fourth one is that which doesn't require inhalation and exhalation.

'Bahyābhyantraviṣayākṣepīcaturthaḥ (*YD.* 2.5)

Now about the practice of *prāṇāyāma* one should be in a

posture comfortable to him whether sitting, standing or sleeping. If you are in sitting or standing posture, you should also apply two knots. First one is *uḍḍīyāna* knot. *Uḍḍīyāna* knot is applied at the level of neck. Bend your neck to the extent that your chin may touch your chest. This knot is must after you have inhaled the air and suspended it, or you may feel giddiness and headache. Second knot is termed as *Jālandhara bandh*. *Jālandhara* knot is applied at the level below the naval on the belly. It is always applied after the breath is exhaled and suspended by tightening the belly. The knowledge of these two knots is quite necessary before we go ahead for the practice of *prāṇāyāma*. Thus having perfected in the application of these two knots, one should start with external *prāṇāyāma* first i.e. slowly exhale the air and hold it therewith as long as you can do comfortably. External *prāṇāyāma* is prescribed first, as with the exhalation of breath all thoughts are also removed out of the mind making it completely thoughtless or passionless. This loosening up of mind also helps in its relaxation.

After the external *prāṇāyāma* is completed, one should observe the internal *prāṇāyāma* by inhaling the air very slowly and holding it inside so long as one can do it comfortably. If you start getting tired of holding it inside, breath out slowly. Before you breath it out completely, hold it in between for the third *prāṇāyāma* i.e. stilled one. This practice will lead one to its higher stage of practice, where motion of breath (inhalation or exhalation is hardly perceptible or say breathing and non-breathing becomes almost identical, which is the fourth *prāṇāyāma*. Thus having perfected *prāṇāyāma* upto its fourth stage, one's mind become fit for concentration and attention.

dhāraṇāsu ca yogyatā manasaḥ (*YD.* 2.53)

On the basis of the foregoing discussion it can easily be informed that practice of *prāṇāyāma* is quite helpful in loosening up of mind, undivided attention, concentration or meditation.

Reference

Yoga Darśana of Patañjali : Tr. in Hindi by Prabhu Dayalu, Published by Sri Venkteshvara Steam Press Bombay, Vikram. Saṁvat 2009.

www.ingramcontent.com/pod-product-compliance
Lightning Source LLC
Chambersburg PA
CBHW021344290326
41933CB00037B/721
* 9 7 8 8 1 8 7 7 1 0 6 6 0 *